Copyright © by Harcourt, Inc.

All rights reserved. No part of this publication may be reproduced or transmitted in any form or by any means, electronic or mechanical, including photocopy, recording, or any information storage and retrieval system, without permission in writing from the publisher.

Requests for permission to make copies of any part of the work should be addressed to School Permissions and Copyrights, Harcourt, Inc., 6277 Sea Harbor Drive, Orlando, Florida 32887-6777. Fax: 407-345-2418.

HARCOURT and the Harcourt Logo are trademarks of Harcourt, Inc., registered in the United States of America and/or other jurisdictions.

Printed in Mexico

ISBN-13: 978-0-15-352730-2
ISBN-10: 0-15-352730-7

1 2 3 4 5 6 7 8 9 10   050   11 10 09 08 07 06

SCHOOL PUBLISHERS

Visit *The Learning Site!* www.harcourtschool.com

Stories Are Not Just in Books

Do you like stories? Many people do. Telling stories is fun. Hearing stories is more fun!

Long ago, there were no books.
But there were stories. All over the
world, people told stories. People
listened to stories. They still do.

Stories That Teach

Some stories teach right and wrong. Others tell about how things were made.

In *The Spider Weaver*, the sun saves a spider from danger. The spider thanks the sun by making clouds.

Many cultures have different stories.
But some stories are almost the same.

Almost every culture has a Cinderella
story. In some cultures, Cinderella is a boy.

Meet a Griot from Africa

People listen to me. What do they hear? They hear songs and music. They hear lots of stories. I know many stories.

African Stories

In Africa, people love stories. They listen. But they are not quiet! They sing. They clap. Sometimes people add to the story.

What are the stories about? They are about my family. They are about my culture. They are about the history of my people.

Who listens to me? Boys do. Girls do. Men do. Women do. All people love stories!

Think and Respond

1. Where do people tell stories?

2. What does the story *The Spider Weaver* explain?

3. What does a griot do?

4. How is hearing a story different from reading a book?

Activity

Make up a story you can tell.
What happens first, next, and last?
Tell your story to your classmates.